Epistle, Osprey

Also by Geri Doran

Sanderlings
Resin

Epistle, Osprey

GERI DORAN

Tupelo Press
North Adams, Massachusetts

Library of Congress Cataloging-in-Publication Data available upon request.
ISBN: 978-1-946482-23-5

Cover and text designed by Josef Beery in Calluna and Bodoni.

Cover art: "Discovering Venn in the Ionian" (2018) by Michael Schultheis.
Used by permission. www.MichaelSchultheis.com

Author photograph: Jay Eads

First edition: August 2019

Tupelo Press
P.O. Box 1767, North Adams, Massachusetts 01247
(413) 664–9611 / editor@tupelopress.org / www.tupelopress.org

Tupelo Press is an award-winning independent literary press that publishes
fine fiction, nonfiction, and poetry in books that are a joy to hold as well as
read. Tupelo Press is a registered 501(c)(3) nonprofit organization, and we
rely on public support to carry out our mission of publishing extraordinary
work that may be outside the realm of the large commercial publishers.
Financial donations are welcome and are tax deductible.

for Hilary

CONTENTS

Island

Blue Marble

Osprey

Epistle, Osprey

ॐ *Island*

ISLAND

For many days I walked to know an island, its tributary paths,
and slipped among the trees to find a hidden beach
or stopped beside the brackish oyster beds
seeking again the feeling—
simply any feeling.

A long time before, feeling had come naturally
and into phrases, shaped and plain,
and that was lost to me,
I feared.

So I walked to know again the textures of the world,
a tangled brier, a hedgerow with its orange
berries, and over here red berries,
and purple ones on branches spiked
like rose-stems.

I came back torn, as when I shear the rosebush in my yard—
and put the berries in a glass already filled
with wildflowers, on a table
softened by fox-red and amber
shoots of reed grass.

Slowly sensation returned. Scrambling over the boulders
on the difficult beach, collecting beach-trash—
Styrofoam, half-empty bottles, cigarette
butts and limp balloons, tampons
from crevices,

some afloat in seawater lounging in rock pools—
I watched my friend billygoat the outcrops,
two black stuffed bags hitched
over his shoulders
lighter than

the slim notebook where he writes down the things
he wishes to remember. How fresh the water
seemed there on the sea-struck, guano'd
rocks, as if neither trash nor rotting fish
could mar

the beachscape of thrown rock, so unearthly
it seemed more earth than anywhere I'd walked—
what salt wind and ocean's pumice
would make clean.

THE OBSERVABLE WORLD

Rain-light saturates the grey-green trees: a blackish hue.
I wake to this from burial sleep, sleep so interred
waking itself is rebirth—

old roots striving for one last greening in the heavier world.
The rain that doesn't come ransoms the sky
and darkly I observe

behind this door of glass where sight alone prevails
(the clouded, fitful mind aswirl)
this longing

to be brought to the skin's sumptuous knowledge, knowing
even as also I am known a covenant of touch
felted and soft—

like the felted, snowy back of the rhododendron leaf
scrupulous in its under-turning, thus secretly
withheld from view.

Seeing is all—and nothing, without this metamorphosis
of touch, the soft, gathering sky at last delivered
into raindrops,

then to the waiting, veiny tenderness of my upturned wrist.
So I move into the world of matter,
matter myself.

Is this the heart's desire, the *completer existence* of the angels?
Are we whole in the sovereign arms of Him,
not the world?

I can't tell the difference. The cedar of Lebanon curls
its branches round, in-holding and grave,
giving shelter

as surely as the overlapped, battened shingles of my roof:
this refuge, a tree more indifferent than consoling;
and yet I find

God himself indifferent, and am consoled.

Sing then, Muse, of the manifest world. Praise the grey-green
weeping downrush of the English birch,
strings of leaf-coin

proclaiming abundance; tell of moss-infused grass
creeping northward toward the blueberry
twigs shocked

out of winter's stupor into flower; sing me into a world
whose constancy intensifies minute by hour:
red-bud heirloom roses

cloaked in their multifoliate dark-green leaves,
tips still closed, protected
by their leafy sepals:

everything is emerald, moss-green, verdigris, grey
but the miraculous red promise of the flowers and berries.

8

Sing, as though in praise the voice could touch the world
and feel, as the finger whorls feel,
the pulse of life;

could dent the velvet bristles on the leaf; and leave its mark
before the world returns
the touch:

visits upon the voice a bodied tremolo, now chorusing—
the birch's chains of leaves
rustling in wind

the rosebuds softly tearing open.

And of the mind's remove? What joinery of knowledge
matters if world and voice become
a single pattern,

twice-shaping—the press upon the one, the other.
No covenant; nothing *held* to be so,
and so confirmed.

One thing, incarnate? To trust two elements divisible
yet bound—this way is known.
Why make of language

and the greening world a unity, dissolvable to one.
Ruddy branches the crape myrtle
flings skyward

define the sky but are not sky, are intricate
as syntax, but do not sound.

ಖಾ

Unvoiced—I cross the threshold of the world
as matter, the glass in shards.

THRESHOLD

First come upon glass, skim-floated on molten tin
& hardened flat. Press a sleepy hand, the narrow pane
shatters. As if in dream, each sliver
gleams its tale of adherence & separation: *I clung to this,*
I was unmade. And glass I am in lover's absence,
shard to his whole, singing molten tin & kiln
singing silica & soda-lime
into transparence—

୫୦

Obsidian the lava glass, mafic & volcano-made, not mineral
in fire but blackened rock, sharpened to a point—to wield, to cut—
blackened as the basalt heart,

what cannot be hard-hearted because it is
already stone.

Stone belies the figure: it is *itself*
& heart the human organ, heart the sign
bears nothing of the weight—
this glass is not transparent but opaque.

INLET

The pathway is silky underfoot. Clover beds
silken like the channel's watery floor, smooth & cool.
Passage beckons like words: *medick trefoil silkworm silt.*
Rootedness has other ways, soft plush enfolding the foot,
tethered to everything: the world a field of clover,
love a field of clover, tang of lemon-mint—
one tiny nubile stem with its four-of-leaves, for luck.

NEAR-IN, THE WORLD

Vestibule portal mudsill latch. Amid tangling grape vine:
wisteria, a spray of honeysuckle over the lintel
portal of scent
sweet gems promising bloom
& beyond the gate, the trellised white secret world
more fragrant & unknowable
mysterious the tenderness of rain on Spanish jasmine
unfathomable wild inference

Can we leave memory & all we know? Can we enter pure
world without our sorrow?

PURE

Sorrowless at the brink *I am standing I am standing*
& the beating breaking heart is mine no longer
it is breaking of its own accord elsewhere & I am here wholly empty
disappearing into the emerald green leaves
the ivory promise of the canna lilies not
the red-budded rose—

ivory & emerald making up a story newly other, birthing
the first world of magnitude & I am *in it*—

neither glass nor of the glass nor through the glass
dark as obsidian or clear as light, just a body in its flesh
unprotected, dreaming itself never broken
never marred

❧ *Blue Marble*

Outer shell of my shell, case hinge & latch—
I dream of salt air next to my skin,
to *be* that air, hymn to enclosure,
hymn to what's withheld.
As if to claim a surer self, a self upright
bound in salt—column & white. Aye, I stay.
Blooming, this continuous wake of day.
Field flowers at woods' edge are delicate,
persist. The morning glory opens
her small trumpet: *not a sound.* The wake
once more is cresting in the Devil's Churn—
creviced, it takes all noise unto itself. Sea
air, thick with salt, with crested wave: sing.
Make morning of this near-complete in-folding.

THE BLUE MARBLE

Arctic snows float in the crystal seas: a flourish
of tempest, clouds intermingling in the blue.
It seems almost water only, and water's frosty vapors.
What's land is pulled across the surface,
tenuously clasped by isthmus here and ribbon there,
like hide stretched for tanning in the ocean's frame.
Bronze swathes of hide amidst a floating blue
the voyagers called the marble. And, yes, it is a little like
verde antique or Connemara limestone or, smaller,
handheld, the child's striped onyx or Jackson swirl.
But this isn't a galactic game of Ringer,
nor is the broad arc of the satellite our interstellar
bid for vantage—we aren't taking rounders
from the universe. This bright blue dot in the everything
is everything—at least everything we'll rightly know,
the sole position from which we'll ever start.

Yet to roam the larger dark and photograph our world
suspended in the sea of black—
perhaps we've been granted a roving caliper
to measure earth's roundness and diameter, the thinness of dry land
we stand on in the swells of space.

You see, it's 1972, the Apollo mission is five hours and six minutes old,
and now we have a picture—the astronauts are taking snaps.
Whole earth in frame, radiant as lapis lazuli.
This blue and white and swirling globe. Ourselves

transposed as though through a telescope, wrong end, into minutiae.
We are invisible. The continental skins we stand on will be discernible,
but not now, not yet. Not until the photograph is turned,
the South Pole restored to the lower hemisphere—
to the place, we tell ourselves, where it belongs.

THE CORK OAK

Motionless as an umber moth in the autumn trees,
motionless as the wave-form pattern of cobblestones in the square,
which appear to travel, and do not—
a figure standing for the end of time, arrested
by shock, forests himself. He draws tree bark and the gloom
close in. Tag-along, the wood sorrel, plumply white,
nods to black and white cobbles with sleepy charm
and lays down her petals. It is good to rest.
In groves, the alder and willow and hazel trees
think nothing of time, and never shall.
All their days, together at gloaming, they dream—
a bracing dream, mysterious to them—
they dream of the cork oak in the deep *montados*, shaved of its bark.

ALL WE ARE NOT

Offshore, beyond the breakwater, past guiding pylons
where the bottom sand drops to depth and the fog collects
dense and more wet—

there in middle distance, nearer to shore than horizon, farther
than the offing, in the constant *medias res* where waves
thicken low and black

and silver above in curls sheared from the surface—
there in movement ceaselessly beating, moon-pulled, savage—
there in the loudest rumble of ocean's dominion

where water intensifies will, will that governs everything
human by contradiction—*all we are not*—
shaming our infidelities great and small, the nothing-human-at-all

of water surges toward landmass, toward us, as if drawn by some
primordial need of hard, geologic plate for its counterpart:
for movement fast and unrelenting, cognate of the rigid mantle.

And we, honeycombed water vialed in pliant flesh, stand between,
cognate of nothing but the mutable way, ourselves obliging
and obdurate by turns, but never completely, and never for long.

NOVEMBER SEA

Today the ocean pulls rage from its depths.

Short walls of obsidian are compelled from below,
roll jagged as broken thick glass, edge-first.

So the waves are sheer-faced as dark glassine.
Westward, they peak, not into foam, into small glaciers.

Less cold, broken off; recalling icebergs all the same.

Water this old, calling up from its past,
calling up from depth—

East, the rollers break onto boulders. None of it
foam lathering onto sand, ebbing away.

On the ferry, pitching atop water like this
I'd thought it volcanic: molten,

just cold. Obvious contradiction.
As is this water: dark-raging, oblivious.

Cold in the old sense, a shoulder turned.
Not worth even a look.

I've wanted to be that contained,
bringing forth nothing

but a wintry chill, and scything,
like ice-glass.

CRAPE MYRTLE IN WINTER

Drawn by the snow-shallow deck of the earth, the iced trees
camber down: crescent branches, a glass-red dangle of berries.
Snow-caked limbs in the alder and sweetgum sheer,
cracking and avalanching. What loss in this great falling
is a delicate, bark-bare tangle of crape myrtle?

The willowy, caramel tangle of myrtle, whose blossoming
once foretold a grief-cold sky. And this white spilling
on the winter terrace, the earth's heart at its hearthstone, all this
muted radiance—snowlight at the midnight hour—
arrives like a foregone conclusion, or precipitous sorrow.

TRAINSONG

Measure of elements, alloyed and moving—
the pressed horns flatten into coal-tar night

and the backyards howl an answer   —Thoroughfare
of the pumped bellows   cigs and novels slung
into knapsacks and hitched to the Union Pacific

Southern Pacific, Great Northern, Pere Marquette—
locomotive, varnish, luggage cars,

flats for freight   coupled, uncoupling

                    —Listen to the pitched incursion,
as the raccoon paused in her searches listens, as misbegotten
star thistle, milk thistle, crown vetch and meadow rue

nod in their proximal sleep, and listen   —Along the grooved
and silver tracks, power lines consonant and overhead
await the hour of passage, and the way thistle

and the children in their tired beds
await a vibration that settles in the cells like a homecoming.
Because movement itself is refuge

when the air's a live current rushing
toward Bismarck, Cheyenne, Fort Dodge

there, or the station after—
to the terminus,

where everything else to come
begins without a lookback, not a flicker
toward the backyard hounds snuffling the night air

or the mothering shells of clapboard and brick, lawns green
or dying, not so much by your leave
as that last buck in your pocket could buy.

Woken by the progress of a midnight freight
or called in their sleepwalk

countrywomen fathom a hum deep as whale-belly,
implacable metal meeting pliable air
with a sharpness within called, urgently,

whistle

not tin whistle, pennywhistle—
not the slit in a blade of quack-grass blown
but this, braiding the dreams of the feverish child,

this siren begat in the quick of night.

LE RÊVE

the dream has shifted landscape
now the burnt-out city
a charred, deserted, no-luck place
that dog packs prowl
becomes this mistake-riddled house
an aftermath more personal—
a home, mine, sometimes large or small
never twice the same
though the feeling is
the feeling of error, grave
or being duped
now in the dream I'm flailing
interior walls damp and fissured
fissures snaking down
dark, furred molds collecting
in subterranean vaults
the stairwells boarded off

how I didn't see
is one theme in the dream
my father now alive, I'm showing him
asking what it means
dark stains, the crumbling hearth
mysterious mud-floored pits below
but as we walk he disappears
next time the house is a mansion
a galley breakfast room

window-ringed
hunches over the basement chambers
hatching rotten timbers
or like last night
the theme again deception
whole rooms were plastered off
(I couldn't have seen
it's not my fault)
in the wall
a narrow hidden cabinet door
opened only onto brick
beside, a peephole
I looked beyond the wall
it was the basement room
risen into sunlight
(though I sensed a furtive darkness)
the mud
had sprouted green

NO EDGE, NO FALLING

Here not waterfalls: scrubby plats of gorse and heather
—a few stray dabs of yellow torn
by stinging winds. We've come
cross rutted track and granite stiles,
along the apertures of fields,
"to stare at some inexplicable old stonework"—
nineteen huddled rocks, nineteen obelisks,
a ring of stones in ancient reformation.

Stark and pricked, wayward:
every footpath this late autumn leads
to stonework ruins draped by fog-ghosts
—the lanky beauties rising cross the heath
not oaks but chimney stacks, hearth-less and chill.
If hungering for anything, we're hungering for fire—
a burst of red to break the endless heath,
a bonfire to warm these cryptic stones.
But listen, in the wind there is a voice—
it isn't only hardship that I offer.

Not only, but ocean dusted blue
which crests against striated crops of granite,
a rocky, disbelieving headland;
and there, beyond, a horizon line so far, so smudged
there is no edge or falling.

after Elizabeth Bishop

CASSITERITE

Tin veins the rock underfoot: two thin black lines border
a whitish, cloudy strip.
Between tussocks of weed, in a cutway through the valley,
its fog-slippery sheen is nothing. Two strands not worth a penny.

Deep in the mines, the streak of cassiterite appeared blue
when it appeared—color sweated from the seeping rock
into the visible,

drilled, hammered, labored in small backbreaking boulders
up to the surface. Blue-black ore
released and smelted, pressed with the *Lamb and Flag*:
Cornish tin for transport.

Near St. Agnes Head, north in the Coastal lode, are hills of blue.
Shoals of pebble
      —discards, in burrow heaps—
cast their gray-blue tint on the grass.

Miners' footpaths crisscross Blowing House Hill to the old stream
below the roofless, grievously
cracked walls of the Blue Hills engine house

      where early miners scavenged tin at water's edge.

Tended, the exhibition center would have traced this scavenging
turned industry—its four thousand years
of sustenance,
        its black-stack ruin.

Ghost histories fleck the land: chimneys, decaying engine houses;
and hidden in long grasses, the circular ironworks that barricade
caving ground-ways.

From the cliff top near Pendeen, I see the red-brown scald of Geevor's
old arsenic works, then squat Levant, and in mind's eye
Botallack, the Crowns perilous on the crags
                                        above a pristine, blue Atlantic.

My mines. Though why I study them, and this fierce coast, eludes me.
Alone in a miner's cottage small for one (it would have held a family),
I turn the vial from the museum shop—
                        hourglass of crystals

in speckled silvery brown. Nothing like the display case's chalk trail:
black ore rubs white,
                        the color of powdered tin.

And this—in this photograph of the last mine to close, South Crofty,
the roadside wall near the shaft's headgear
                                is gray galvanized by green
like leaf-shadowed lichen.
Stark against it, hand-painted white—one freighted line:

Cornish lads are fishermen, and Cornish lads are miners too,
    but when the fish and tin are gone what are the Cornish boys to do?

THE RIVER HERE

Sounds, early mornings, like rain—
has hollows in the rushing, like rain, bolting the small
rock ledge, the river's modest rapids that later,
in sunshine, will fern-ridge and canopy
into deep brindled shade; here in the *argoat*,
thick of the woods, what remains of forest
greens like this, dark and dull in the morning,
sun-marbled cloister as day wears on.
And worn, is that the word, for mills made of schist
and granite, centuries old and lacking work,
for gaping churches tamed by tourists
to the size of a camera lens?

This river is split, *Kerustang* moving quiet
towards the millrace, greenly clear, grasses
under glass swaying languid and outstretched;
K. furioso channeled through square-cut sluiceways
onto rock beds, where granite boulders lead
to step-work ledges, so this branch rustles more.
Below me, below the old millworks, the two rejoin,
one tousled from its fall over the gate, one hustling
to find its way back.

Is this, then, where passion's gone?
Old Catholic, this country, and wouldn't one know,
flecked with chapels, forsaken calvaries—
what thrived in field, ground upon the millstone;

in belief, marked with a cross.
The end of passion's not crucifixion,
it's this—
a Christ broken-off at the torso
high on a pocked stone beside a road-rimmed forest,
a forest once boundless and lush.

ဆ

Let's set the crosses spinning, see where Christ's right hand
and Fortune meet. The roulette of history:
Roman, Celt, Frank and Englishman invade the Gaul;
now it's France but *Breiz Izel*, too, Breton
through to granite, in the voice and in the land.
A thousand pardons for a thousand saints—
a holy tincture dyes the ancient place.

This holy *and* this green, and where a cross
stands stark on drier ground: no less. Hedges
of wild hydrangea square the fields, crops are cultivated,
hay reaped and baled, the farmer brings potatoes
to the market and labors on.

ဆ

What remains when passion's sluiced away
from its source? Chapels, empty, moss taking
the floors as it takes the river-rocks and calvaries.
And there it all is, locked and waiting;

a woman in the village has the key.
Sly Pound knew the score, but missed by a tick:
what you lovest still is here:
it *is* the dross.

NOT THE STIGMATA

⁊

For on the palm, no evidence remained. Shoeblack—
rubbed across the fat padding of the thumb. From the hoe,
slivers of worn wood, worked in. These, then the saw blade
one day and pink coloring the fresh sawdust. In a manner,
kind—for what might have been the hand itself was just
one finger, a small price—not sign so much as an early
reclamation: *This I shall take back one day.* Blithe child—
did you not see in your father's wounded hand some
flickering of what could be mistaken—and what taken?

⁊

For red bloomed in his left hand chaliced in his right,
a paint rag sopping blood. Of faith you saw no mark,
just flesh scattered in the shavings—could this
be reconstructed into a legend, or devotion? Not
a moment's wayward thought but something constant
consecrated. *For I shall never leave you* was less hearsay
than the solemn vow proclaimed by blood. In your hand,
child, the workman's hand, one finger shorn—
soft now upon the sheet, his untouched palm dying in your own.

THE DEATH BOX

Kerepesi Cemetery, Budapest

Atlas shouldering,
the globe-world concaved deep into his back,
would have marked a stately grief. Instead the sculptor chose
these pall bearers and the coffin,
an instant of
utter exertion: the stone box straining
down toward its earth-magnet,
four men pitched against gravity,
the stone of the men
unequal to the stone casket. Theirs is the granite musculature
of long-practiced indenture;
the box, dead weight of abandonment and bone.
Who sleeps
beneath the brown ivy, dried leaves
obscuring the stone wish: *P X.*
Is he son or friend—the one whose slim back narrows
to a small ravine darkened by shadow
as he heaves?
And the other, looking away and down, the coffin
squared on his stooped back—
is that simply to allay the weight?

THE HEIFER MAIDEN

In the lover's account, she grazed her way home,
her four legs a tired thickness above her rounded hooves—
and Argus let her, *what risk?* She weighed near fifty stone.
Home along the river's bank she nuzzled grasses
rippling in their slick green skins, and watched her sisters
cool in the water, fresh, knee-thin. What she
would never be again. Was there sweet relief
to know no god would chase her now, this tonnage
not a curse? Her white, her weight, the shape to reconcile—
Spurred, she moved, then moved again
from meadow grass to rivulet
no longer sought or seeking.
Some call this bliss.
She grazed across the lands, fattened onward
to the Nile, blue refuge, and there the gods forgot her.
Oh, they changed her back.
The leathery hide softened to pink skin. She felt
her hands, ran fingers over tree bark
to touch again with pleasure, not as itch.
Her two legs took their human shape, but heavier.
She had a little belly now.
And rarely spoke. The poet joked: she was afraid she'd moo.
No—just, now she had the care
of what she'd carried: dimensions no trickery
could undo.

THE RED FOX

He appeared and escaped like a slipknot—
a flash, one turning feint, then air.
In the village street his red-orange
seemed at first miraculous
then unknowable, then drear.
He brought no luck.
—A rural fox, no hounds, no dare.

FISH LIGHT

> We are afloat
> On our dreams as on a barge made of ice,
> Shot through with questions and fissures of starlight
> —*John Ashbery*

Or the barge is cast iron, blackly dense in undreaming waters,
where the libertine soul bedazzles her intimate
towards frothy daylight, *come now*, she says, *don't be
leaden.*
       But he in herself is no vagabond weight,
sweet paradox love—and oh how he stays,
heavifying here to the nth of here,
the darkwaters lit by a make-believe fish
silvering through a seaway that doesn't exist.

EVER AFTER

Blue as prophecy, the pale bells shiver in spring wind,
woodland Cassandras before the turn. Gold in the green barley,
fields billowing around a shut Breton cottage.
Autumn's scuttering leaf-drop. Given these, should winter
have disquieted me? I study tarot, tea leaves, bones,
swirls in the azure paint, your silence—*infinite*—the runes.

BLOOD FROM STONE

As when the matter is taken in hand
but the heart refused
and the good muscle begins to thicken;
or when the mountain, ceremonious in the early moonlight,
loosens one small rock to the waiting creek;
then the yeasted bread rising and cracking,
the red-handled pump drawing up water brown
with rust—
as when we are given, but not enough.

EVER THINE

Except the husbanding heart gleans on, gathering
autumn's sienna, burnt yellow. And the music of constancy
gives way to a solitude brimming, so that it seems the genesis
of life itself: the moment just before, the verge.
Infused, welling, I tender these: crackling maple,
birch and hazel leaves. Once-beloved,
I tender them now to you.

QUANTUM

Ample is the quantum of darkness framed by the midnight window.
Or the quantum of scent accorded to each bud:
the butterknife tips of the paperwhite blooming into teacups.
In memory, a measurement tending always toward confinement.
By definition, a singularity, though shared among, as in
your portion, mine. Like a tiny burst of upright joy, size of a fingertip,
this dark-minted first hour of a new year.

MEASURE, MIDAS

For weight of gold, the dip of the polished scale is just—
for love, the breath's swift return by starling
I close my eyes
I close my eyes and still—
your curved cheekbone arches toward my chaste kiss

DWELL

Gravelly in the well are echoes, whetted stone to stone;
where the moss is thickest, there they soften.
Threading toward the aquifer, the column is dark
and dank—a conduit once for clarifying water.
Now it's boarded at the top, the bucket used for flowers.
Impatiens. Forget-me-nots. Even the flowerpots chide,
and redly make their brooding little flourish.

ॐ

From inside, looking out the skylight window,
there are mountains shadowed, just there,
blue-black shadows fronting an ultramarine sky
side-lit by the moon—so as it fills and thins
the color deepens and recants. Sleep then, love.
When you wake in a downy blur, you'll see
no mountain there. Just green treetops
you mistook for crests; a range floats-in by night,
at daybreak disappears.

ॐ

Awake to the river's noises: sloshy unraveling,
constant as an engine, from the open arched window;
below, a whisper as the water runs the millrace,
contained as a heart, tapping the narrow walls.
These are runic sounds, if I divine them. Runic,
too, are the slate-blue floorboards, patterns

swirled in their paint, and patterns in the laying
of the rocks for walls, for window-wells and ledges.
At every turn a mystery solved, if I could grasp it.

ॐ

Jailbird. Just how is soul to dwell in something
kin to ease? A woman tends the cottage near the ancient well,
plants lilac next to primrose, impatiens in the bucket.
These root here, and she. Another, migrant, perches
on rotting slats of the wooden footbridge,
the water inscrutable in the sheltered glade.

ॐ

To each soul, perhaps, a method. Behold the lilies
of the field. Behold the golden sea of barley, swaying
in the wind, its drying tops and undershoots of green.
We move, we dwell. We cast our rune stones
with a fervent wish.

Osprey

EPISTLE, OSPREY

Beyond the catch of sunlight on clustered rose hips
is the way this letter began, years ago, before shifting
to the shadows moving along the mason's stonework—
I sat at the garden's iron table, watching
a magpie's two-toned flit in the hedgerow,
and waited for . . . what? . . . some purifying
figure from this element to catch in language,
metaphysics turned perception, turned fire.
How impractical it all was, each moment—
and yet how worldly. Place names balanced
on the tongue: *Penwith, Pendeen.*
Love was restored, but in the bygone sense
of simple pleasure, common feeling. To get past
the body's need, or the heart's—
I hadn't imagined the world could be enough.

Now when people ask, I point to the osprey's nest
above the trellised bridge.

Because it distracts, that other strand we call the world—
by which I mean now temporal, secular, the *fray*
happening in human life, from the morning's spilled coffee
onto a neatly laundered skirt to hospital days in their blur
—medications, creams, forms, nurses, diagnoses,
the priest severe in black, all slurried into equivalent,
meaningless things.
                    While the heart contends
with death's leviathan fact.

And it's false to say the orange-red shivering leaves
offer recompense, though looking out on them
calms my trembling.

Perhaps that is the lesson in love. So is this osprey,
disregarding the humans below though surely alert to us.
She hungers, feeds, then hurtles to her high, thistled home.

STARTLING, THESE OCEAN-LINERS OF AIR

With their Stevens-weight of sense hovering over
the manmade lake and its ration of shells.

Polished, almost cherubic, these cumulus-pooling sheers
park in the sky on their dark, flat bottoms—
sky never clouded so, rarely this amply occupied—
a midseason swell of luxury on tarnished-silver hulls.

Luxury of light-infused vapor, resplendent altars
of high breath—

belled curves luminesce like the eagle's fletched dive
for the silver-green dappled bass.

It cancels the morning's instruction against the pastoral.
Arches into the natural as a fish flexed in talons.
Silver-green bent dying into sky.

Ideas sway in the wake of tail feathers—magnificent
transference, a shimmering, as material
as the rowers *ahh*-ing below in their spiny shells.

Water drops have chilled to incandescent cloud bank,
an eagle ascends with its broken feast.
All is limpid.

Can you see? The world recomposes
around its menace.

MADRE DE DIOS

To return to things themselves is to return to that world
which precedes knowledge, of which knowledge always *speaks*,
and in relation to which every scientific schematization is an abstract
and derivative sign-language, as is geography in relation to
the countryside in which we have learnt beforehand what a forest,
a prairie or a river is.

　　　　　　　　—*Maurice Merleau-Ponty*

Because we see in him our image, he is made
　　portal to the observable world,
　　　　our lens a boy stationed

high in a branch, looking on—
　　casual in the evening dusk-light,
　　　　his lean boy's shape silhouetted,

the boughs and leaves silhouetted,
　　in lustrous sky whose shelterlings
　　　　we cannot know.

We are stilled for the moment
　　by wonder: how at ease he is
　　　　on the thin high branch,

which barely bows under his weight.
　　Look how he surveys,
　　　　arms spread to steady himself,

to embrace the transept, his view kingly
　　above the Heath, this river child
　　　　of the Madre de Dios.

We would fashion him, yes, a boy,
    spying on a suburban yard, stone
        to toss squeezed beneath two fingers—

but for proportion, the camera's rendering
    of arm, torso, branch and leaf
        mangling our intent

to make familiar the unknown:
    smudge of the nearer leaf-growth,
        branches crooking skyward.

A whole is formed, a trapezium
    of tree limbs continuous with a body
        not human,

the arms, we see now, all wrong,
    the upper body foreshortened,
        as was our understanding.

                        ℰℐ

The original is unfaithful to the translation
                              —*Jorge Luis Borges*

Such lightness. As if only a feather's weight—
the spider monkey, now himself,

balances in the tree canopy, over a river
not mine to take

by sight or misconstruing. For this invention
of likeness is no less

a falsehood than a fishhook elegant
in the curved and coiled wires of its capture—

a piranha's gold and silver scales
speckling like diamonds

around translucent diaphanous gills—
all suspended

in perfect calm
over the perfect midnight blue of the water.

I trace the hook to the human hand
trace correspondences of shape—

searching for my world
in this

breathtaking *untranslatable* one.

ɛͻ

Mar Dulce, sweet sea—river sea
with your thousand tributaries—
what language
is your coursing?

Cocha or oxbow, *playa*, sandbank:
   no matter. *Rio de la Canela,*
      grand Amazon:
         you are yourself

original water-vein, your glacial
   wellhead marked
      by a wooden cross for all
         you must bear:

current, torrent—life world
   of millennia. Rain, in deluge.
      Forest, thicket of green—
         and that one

blue dragonfly the able photographer
   held, for one instant,
      toward eternity.
         This is

hisses the steam-rising morning;
   the sunbittern and the walking palm,
      Inga blossom and sloth.
         This will be

(untethered piranha,
   sweet river-mother of god)
      all you ever need.

BLACK MARBLE

Constancy? Tonight the peerless stars atone
for countless pinched & starless nights. We ride currents

of royal blue on our continental crust, safe as houses,
safe *in* houses that perch on plains & hillsides—

or grip the sand & face the coastal tide, like seabirds
fierce into the gale. This hold—the lithic earth below

our feet—grounds & keeps us. Metamorphic rock
spans down, hardly fragile, yet when sleep declines

to come, I recall the earth we've known these forty years,
a waif, transformed in space—& lonelier than Lucifer mid-fall—& how

the frosted breath of clouds obscured bronze fleets of land
so thin they seemed the barest scraps of hide. Or something more

like wafers of flint & splintered rock, our tiny rafts—
we their castaways.

Polestar, we say, meaning one who guides us, & we navigate by stars,
wish upon them, name constellations after gods

& pouty boys—& by dint of that know ourselves substantial.
But this laptop's glowing portal, companion in my wakeful nights,

spins me from the photographed *Blue Marble* to these
night versions, each a seeming vision of the stars, moon-arc'd

by a protective curve of light. They are not stars, but city lights.
Whispered myths, human comedies winking in the black—

disobedience, splendid love affairs, heroics, all ephemeral &—
That & all our quest is mirrored back.

క

NOTES

"Island"   Reading Louise Glück and James Wright gave me my bearings here. The poem is for Nate Malinowski.

"The Observable World" responds in part to David Abram's *The Spell of the Sensuous* and his reading of Maurice Merleau-Ponty. "Completer existence" is from Rilke's First Duino Elegy, translated by William Gass.

"No Edge, No Falling" quotes and takes up Elizabeth Bishop's "Questions of Travel."

"Fish Light"   Backtalk, after a fashion, to John Ashbery's "My Erotic Double."

"Cassiterite"   The graffito on the mine wall remained long after South Crofty closed. Its origin was the song "Cornish Lads" by Roger Bryant.

"The River Here"   *Kerustang* is the name of a river in central Brittany; the second name, *K. furioso,* is an invention.

"Madre de Dios"   For Sam Abell and Torben Nissen, whose photographs of the Amazon River and rainforest were catalysts for this poem. Epigraphs come from Maurice Merleau-Ponty's *Phenomenology of Perception* (translated by Colin Smith) and Jorge Luis Borges's "On William Beckford's *Vathek*" (translated by Eliot Weinberger in *Selected Non-Fictions*).

ACKNOWLEDGMENTS

Poems from this volume first appeared in the following journals, sometimes in different versions or with older titles. I am grateful to the editors.

The Arkansas International: "Cassiterite"; *Birmingham Poetry Review*: "Quantum" and "Trainsong"; *Connotation Press/A Poetry Congeries*: "Startling, These Ocean-Liners of Air"; *The Harlequin*: "Blood from Stone"; *New England Review*: "Black Marble," "Madre de Dios," and "No Edge, No Falling"; *Ninth Letter*: "Not the Stigmata" and "The Observable World: A Sequence" ("The Observable World," "Threshold," "Inlet," "Near-In, the World," and "Pure"); *Southwest Review*: "Crape Myrtle in Winter" and "The Heifer Maiden"; *The Stinging Fly*: "The River Here"; *Subtropics*: "Fish Light" and "[Outer shell of my shell]"; and *The Yale Review*: "All We Are Not."

"No Edge, No Falling" was reprinted on *Poetry Daily*.

Lighthouse Works, James Merrill House, Maison Dora Maar, and Can Serrat kindly welcomed me during the completion of this book. My thanks to all for secluded writing desks, beautiful surroundings, and generous financial support.

Many thanks to the Creative Arts Council and the College of Arts and Sciences at the University of Oregon for gifts of time; to the Oregon Arts Commission for an Individual Artist Fellowship, which supported my travels in Brittany;

and to the staff of Geevor Tin Mine Museum for sharing their knowledge of Cornish mines. My deep gratitude to Carolyn Altman, David Bradley, Karen Ford, William Logan and George Rowe for friendship and support while I wrestled with this book; to Martin Nesbit and Lucy Johnson for unsurpassable hikes in distant places; and to Jim Schley for his fine editorial hand. *Epistle, Osprey* wouldn't exist but for the good offices of Jeffrey Levine, David Rossitter, Josef Beery, and everyone at Tupelo Press—no *thank you* is sufficient, but mine is truly given.

This book is for my sister, Hilary Kay Doran, with love.

CPSIA information can be obtained
at www.ICGtesting.com
Printed in the USA
FFHW022218190719
53710708-59405FF